GREEN BERETS

by Martin Gitlin

Content Consultant
Mitchell A. Yockelson
Professor, United States Naval Academy

CORE
LIBRARY

Published by ABDO Publishing Company, PO Box 398166, Minneapolis, MN 55439. Copyright © 2013 by Abdo Consulting Group, Inc. International copyrights reserved in all countries. No part of this book may be reproduced in any form without written permission from the publisher. The Core Library™ is a trademark and logo of ABDO Publishing Company.

Printed in the United States of America,
North Mankato, Minnesota
112012
012013

Editor: Lauren Coss
Series Designer: Becky Daum

Cataloging-in-Publication Data
Gitlin, Martin.
 Green Berets / Martin Gitlin.
  p. cm. -- (Great warriors)
Includes bibliographical references and index.
ISBN 978-1-61783-723-4
1. United States. Army. Special Forces--Juvenile literature. 2. Special forces (Military science)--Juvenile literature. I. Title.
356/.167/0973--dc22

                                              2012946369

Photo Credits: Samuel King/US Army, cover, 1; Scott Nelson/Getty Images, 4; Efrem Lukatsky/AP Images, 9, 11; Red Line Editorial, 10, 29; APTN/AP Images, 12; Hubert Erb/AP Images, 14; Ralph Crane/Time Life Pictures/ Getty Images, 17; AP Images, 19, 20; Laurnet Rebours/AP Images, 22; Greg Mathieson/Mai/Time Life Pictures/Getty Images, 24; Gabriel Mistral/ Getty Images, 26; Staff Sgt. Russell Klika/US Army, 28; US Army, 31; Ann Heisenfelt/AP Images, 32; Patrick Aventurier/Gamma-Rapho/Getty Images, 34; Sgt. Rob Summitt/US Army/AP Images, 36; Brennan Linsley/AP Images, 39, 45; Achmad Ibrahim/AP Images, 40

CONTENTS

CHAPTER ONE

TAKING ON THE TALIBAN

It was the fall of 2001. Special Forces Operational Detachment Alpha (ODA) 595 was in the heart of enemy territory. This time, that enemy was the Taliban. The Taliban was a violent religious group. It had controlled Afghanistan since 1996. The group had killed many civilians in its rise to power. It had also allowed terrorist groups to live and train in Afghanistan. One of these groups, Al Qaeda, had

A Green Beret rides a horse in Afghanistan. Green Berets often try to blend in with their surroundings.

A Teams

A Green Beret's job is to blend into his surroundings. Because of this, Green Berets are split into 12-man Operational Detachment Alpha teams, also known as A Teams. Each group has two leaders—a commanding officer and the warrant officer, or second in command. The rest of the team is made up of people with special skills, such as knowledge of medicine or weapons. Everyone on the team has other skills as well as their specialty skills. This means the A Team can split into two groups if needed.

attacked the United States just a few months earlier.

The 12 men of ODA 595 were a Special Forces A-Team unit. Like all US Army Special Forces members, they were known as Green Berets. They were named for the green berets they wore as part of their uniforms. The team's mission was to make the area where they were landing unsafe for terrorists.

Danger Ahead

The team's first mission was to make contact with the Northern Alliance. This was a group of Afghan rebels who opposed the Taliban. The rebels would be the

Green Berets' allies. The Green Berets met with the rebels' leader, General Abdul Rashid Dostum. He wanted to capture the Afghan city Mazar-e Sharif. The Taliban had controlled the city for the past three years. The Green Berets would help him.

It was a tough journey to Mazar-e Sharif. The Green Berets traveled dangerous mountain trails on horseback. For some on the team, it was their first time on a horse. Sometimes the Green Berets and the rebels slept in caves. Other nights they slept outside. It was fall in Afghanistan, and the weather was cold. Food ran low. The Green Berets shared what little food they had with the rebels. Green Berets were trained to overcome the toughest conditions.

The Green Berets and the rebels were traveling through Taliban territory. Each day they faced battles against the Taliban. The odds were not in the Green Berets' favor. The Taliban outnumbered the Northern Alliance rebels. The rebels' weapons were not as good as the Taliban's. During the day the Green

Why Mazar-e Sharif?

Mazar-e Sharif was an important Afghan city for many reasons. Whoever controlled the city had a big advantage. Mazar-e Sharif was on important supply routes. By taking the city, the Green Berets would cut off weapons and supplies coming to the Taliban. The US forces would be able to control these supply routes. Aid, supplies, and weapons could now come to the US forces and their allies. The city also had a military base and an airport. The airport would give US troops a place to land their aircraft inside Afghanistan.

Berets and the rebels chased the Taliban through the mountains until dark fell. Before long they were just outside of Mazar-e Sharif.

The Taliban made their last stand on the morning of November 9. One group of the Green Berets had the high ground of a mountain pass. The Taliban fighters had the low ground. The Taliban had covered the pass with hidden mines. The mines killed many rebels. The Taliban fired rocket launchers at the Green Berets and the rebels. But the Green Berets and the rebels fought back.

Mazar-e Sharif is home to a large mosque, or place of Muslim worship. It also has an airport and a military base.

Meanwhile, other teams of Green Berets had been heading to Mazar-e Sharif from a different direction. Rebels also accompanied these Green Berets. On the morning of November 10, these teams met up with the Green Berets who were with General Dostum. Together the groups had enough weapons and soldiers to take on the Taliban. They moved into the outskirts of the city. There they took the military base and airport.

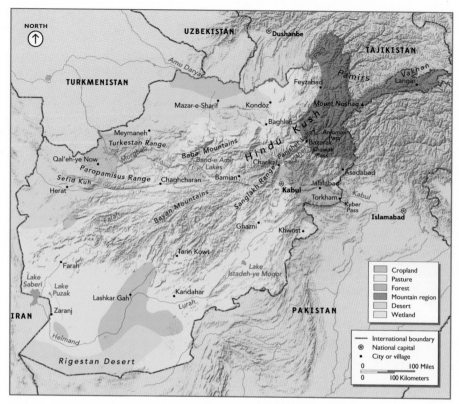

Afghanistan

This map shows Afghanistan's geologic features. What areas would be difficult for a large army to get into? What areas would be easy? What areas of the country would be best suited for Green Beret teams? How does this map help you understand the text better?

Liberating the City

The Green Berets expected a counterattack by the Taliban. But the counterattack didn't come. By the time the Green Berets and their allies got to the city, they had forced most of the Taliban to retreat. The

A Green Beret visits a school for girls in Mazar-e Sharif. Green Berets work hard to gain the trust of the people in the regions they are working in.

Green Berets and the rebels met little resistance as they made their way into the city. Many of the Taliban who stayed in Mazar-e Sharif were quickly taken as prisoners. It was the first US victory over the Taliban. The US forces and their allies now controlled the most important city in northern Afghanistan.

A Green Beret says goodbye to General Dostum near Mazar-e Sharif.

The Green Berets had defeated the enemy by gaining the trust of the Afghan soldiers and people. And they had defeated the enemy through their skills as fighters. But ODA 595 would not stay in the city for long. Shortly after arriving in the city, ODA 595's time in Mazar-e Sharif was over. The Green Berets were on to their next mission.

Sergeant Will was the communications sergeant for ODA 595. In a 2002 interview about the capture of Mazar-e Sharif, he described how Green Berets are different from other units of the US military:

> I think the key point in this entire thing is that Special Forces has always been able to do this mission, which is to go in, work with, train, advise, fight alongside of an indigenous force effectively enough to lead them to victory. What we do, in doing that, is we do, we keep the regular Army, which are just our regular soldiers, out of conflict. We let someone take care of their own problems. We help them, we assist them to do that. The key thing here is that . . . the reins were let loose. And we were allowed to act how we've been trained. We were allowed to be the fighters that we are, free thinking, spontaneous. And we did it. We spread out. We did exactly what we were trained to do. And that was victory. And that is what Special Forces does.
>
> Source: "Interview: U.S. Special Forces ODA 595." Frontline. WGBH Educational Foundation, 2002. Web. Accessed September 14, 2012.

What's the Big Idea?

Take a close look at Sergeant Will's words from the interview. What is his main idea? What evidence does he use to support his main point? Come up with a few sentences explaining how Sergeant Will uses evidence to support his main idea.

CHAPTER TWO

PLANTING THE SEEDS FOR GREATNESS

In the early 1940s, the United States was caught up in World War II (1939–1945). The country joined with Great Britain, France, and other countries to fight against Germany and its allies. In 1942 President Franklin D. Roosevelt created the Office of Strategic Services (OSS) to help the war effort. The OSS's mission was to gain information

Green Berets have been an important part of the US Armed Forces for more than 60 years.

A History of Special Forces

American warriors carried out special combat duties 200 years before any soldier put on a green beret. During the French and Indian War (1754–1763), guerilla warriors known as Rogers's Rangers dashed around swamps and woods to track the enemy. A band of Confederate soldiers led by John S. Mosby, known as Mosby's Raiders, used unconventional tactics in the Civil War (1861–1865). Other special forces warriors helped the United States and its allies defeat Germany in World War II.

about the enemy. It would also sabotage the enemy whenever possible.

The United States and its allies won the war in 1945. In 1952 the army created the 10th Special Forces Group. Its mission was to infiltrate, or sneak, deep into enemy-occupied territory.

Aaron Bank was an important OSS soldier. He took command of the new group. The first Special Forces unit was launched in Fort Bragg, North Carolina, on June 19, 1952. Bank picked the toughest and most talented soldiers he could find.

The 10th Special Forces Group organized and trained guerilla fighting units inside an enemy's territory.

Helping Others Help Themselves

In 1953 the first group of Special Forces was sent overseas. These soldiers traveled to Germany. During World War II, many Eastern Europeans had been shipped to Germany. They remained in Western Europe after the war had ended to avoid living under Communist rule in Eastern Europe. They wanted to create a resistance movement in the Communist countries of Eastern Europe.

The United States was also opposed to Communism. These Special Forces soldiers would train the Eastern European rebels. The resistance failed. But the Special Forces would be included in future US Army plans.

Special Forces in Vietnam

By 1954 a nation halfway around the world was in the middle of a civil war. North Vietnam was fighting to unify the nation under Communist rule. A rebel group called the Vietcong supported the North Vietnamese. South Vietnam was fighting to keep its democratic government.

In 1957 Special Forces teams went to the island of Okinawa, Japan. Their job was train the South Vietnamese army to fight against the Vietcong and the North Vietnamese army.

In 1961 John F. Kennedy became president of the United States. Kennedy soon approved the official headgear for all US Army Special Forces. The soldiers were now known as the Green Berets. In 1961 Kennedy sent more Green Berets to South

President John. F. Kennedy called for the US Army's Special Forces to wear the green berets for which they would be known.

As US involvement in Vietnam grew, so did the fighting for the Green Berets.

Vietnam. These Green Berets would act as trainers and advisers.

Training Grounds

Vietnam was a perfect training ground for the Green Berets. The war was not fought in the way most Americans were used to. It was not fought on traditional battlefields. Instead US soldiers in Vietnam were forced to fight in jungles and mountains. Their enemies were trained to make surprise attacks. The US soldiers hardly ever saw the enemy against which they were fighting.

The Vietnam War gave the Green Berets a chance to work with Vietnamese locals. They trained the Vietnamese to fight the rebels. In return the Vietnamese taught the Green Berets about their enemy, their land, and their language.

More Missions

The Green Berets were able to use the strategies they had learned in Vietnam in another conflict during the 1980s. During this time, the Central American country of El Salvador was in the middle of a civil war.

Lang Vei

In 1968, 24 Green Berets and 400 Vietnamese villagers were defending the South Vietnamese camp Lang Vei. On February 6, they realized that several North Vietnamese army tanks were rolling toward the camp. North Vietnamese soldiers were close behind. The North Vietnamese began attacking Lang Vei. The Green Berets and their forces were overwhelmed. But they fought back. Even after North Vietnamese soldiers had broken into the camp, the Green Berets and their allies kept fighting. The North Vietnamese captured Lang Vei. But because of the Green Berets' efforts, many Green Berets and South Vietnamese escaped. Every Green Beret involved was honored for great service.

Green Berets played an important role in liberating Kuwait from Iraqi forces.

A Communist government was trying to take over the military government of the small country.

The US government sent Green Berets to El Salvador in 1981. The Green Berets trained the El Salvadoran military to fight the Communist forces.

In 1990 Green Berets were called into action once again. Iraqi dictator Saddam Hussein and his military had invaded and terrorized neighboring Kuwait. Countries around the world were troubled by Iraq's invasion.

The United States led the effort to liberate Kuwait. The Green Berets were there to help. They conducted search and rescue missions. They watched the border. They trained Kuwaitis. These duties and more helped bring a quick victory.

The Green Berets had become quite familiar with their mission by that time. They were much more than a fighting force. They were teachers. They were students of other lands and other cultures. They were friends to allies of the United States. They tried to be the best the US military had to offer.

FURTHER EVIDENCE

Take another look at Chapter Two. What are its main points? Can you find supporting evidence to back up these points? The Web site below describes the Special Forces. What new information does the Web site give? Find a few quotes from the Web site. Do these quotes support the evidence you found in the chapter? Or do they make a new point?

What Are the Special Forces?
www.pbs.org/wgbh/pages/frontline/shows/campaign/ground/specialforces.html

CHAPTER THREE

EARNING A GREEN BERET

G reen Berets need to be smart. They need to be physically tough. They must be able to work well with others. They need to be able to make quick decisions with little guidance. This involves a lot of training.

Qualifying

The training to become a Green Beret is extremely difficult. The training is only open to men between the

Not just anyone can become a Green Beret. Many people who want to be Green Berets are turned down before the training even begins.

Only men between the ages of 20 and 30 are eligible to become Green Berets. They must be physically and mentally tough.

ages of 20 and 30. Trainees must have graduated high school. They are screened to make sure they can earn a secret security clearance.

The first part of Green Beret training is a demanding physical test. To even have a chance of being selected, trainees must finish a two-mile

(3.2 km) run in less than 14 minutes. They need to do 100 sit-ups and 100 push-ups in two minutes each. Only about one-third of trainees pass the physical test.

Trainees who pass the physical test enter a 24-day Special Forces Assessment and Selection (SFAS) course. The course takes place at Fort Bragg, North Carolina. The training for SFAS is very difficult. The training includes running, swimming, and obstacle courses. Trainees learn to march while carrying heavy packs. The course tests leadership and teamwork qualities. Trainees who pass

A Tough Course

During the second week of the SFAS physical fitness test, Green Beret candidates must complete a 1.5-mile (2.4 km) obstacle course. They must also finish a navigation course of more than 11 miles (18 km). The rough terrain includes hills and water. Trainees do the course at night without a flashlight. They must work alone. They carry a heavy backpack. They must finish the course no matter the weather. Each trainee gets three chances to complete the course. It is the longest navigation course in the US armed service that is carried out alone.

During SFQC, trainees are put to the test to see if they have what it takes to be a Green Beret.

SFAS can move on to the Special Forces Qualification Course (SFQC). SFQC has five phases, phase II through phase VI.

SFQC

Phase II tests an individual's skills. Trainees learn how to operate in a small unit. They learn land navigation. They also learn how to use weapons.

Position	Number on Team	Primary Role
Commanding Officer	1	Also known as the captain. Leads the A Team. Organizes the mission.
Warrant Officer	1	Takes command if the commanding officer is absent or no longer able to lead. Leads one of the teams in the event that the A Team splits into two groups.
Weapons Sergeant	2	Expert at using and maintaining various US and foreign weapons.
Engineering Sergeant	2	Expert at combat engineering, including knowledge of destroying structures, explosives, construction, land mines, and more.
Medical Sergeant	2	Medical expert, including knowledge of trauma medicine, veterinary medicine, dentistry, and more.
Communications Sergeant	2	Expert at operating many kinds of communications gear.
Intelligence Sergeant	1	Collects and evaluates information about the enemy and foreign lands.
Operations Sergeant	1	Helps organize and train the team, and makes sure it has the necessary supplies and weapons; supports the team's commander.

Positions on an A Team

This chart shows the roles on a typical Green Beret A Team and what the men with those roles do. The teams can be altered as needed depending on a mission. Why might an A Team need to change its makeup for certain missions? How does having a better idea of the makeup of an A Team help you understand a Green Beret's training?

Phase III places Green Beret candidates into the areas in which they are best suited. If they graduate to the Special Forces, each Green Beret will have a specific role on an A Team.

Robin Sage

Robin Sage is a complicated war game that has taken place near Ramseur, North Carolina, since 1974. Robin Sage takes place in a fictional country called the People's Republic of Pineland. The goal of Robin Sage is to help rebels free Pineland from a cruel ruler. Locals act in the game. Some are friends to the trainees. Others are enemies. But the trainees never know whom they can trust. The scenarios in which the trainees participate are based on real events experienced by actual Green Berets.

In phase IV, trainees learn more about the Green Berets and unconventional warfare operations. Trainees participate in a realistic unconventional warfare scenario called Robin Sage. During the scenario, soldiers are tested on how well they make decisions and whether or not they complete their mission.

Phase V focuses on language training. The course takes between

During Robin Sage, soldiers are split into teams. Each soldier must work in his team to complete realistic guerilla warfare missions.

two and three months to complete, depending on the difficulty of the language. Soldiers also receive more combat training in Phase V.

Phase VI is the final phase of training. Trainees go through a Survival, Evasion, Resistance, and Escape (SERE) course. In the SERE course, trainees learn survival skills. They also learn how to avoid being captured and what to do if they are captured.

After completing the SFQC, a soldier finally earns the honor of wearing a green beret.

Putting on the Green Beret

Green Beret training is tough. A soldier can graduate only after finishing all five phases of training. Then he is assigned to a detachment, or unit. Finally each soldier is given his green beret. His training might be over, but the hardest part of being a Green Beret is still to come. Next the soldier is sent into the field.

Former soldier and author Dick Couch wrote the following passage about Green Berets in his book, *Chosen Soldier*:

> He must be tough and he must know how to fight, but there's more than professional military skill and physical toughness involved. The Special Forces warrior requires a unique mind-set. We cannot win this insurgent war without the help of the villagers, tribes, and townspeople who represent [a potential safe home] for insurgents.
>
> Warriors who understand other cultures, and who can live among them and gain their trust, have value beyond measure. These men are hard to find and, once found, must be rigorously trained and tested. Special Forces training is all about finding talented men who have adaptive, creative minds. . . . Physical toughness is a requisite; mental agility is essential.
>
> Source: Dick Couch. Chosen Soldier: The Making of a Special Forces Warrior. New York: Crown Publishing, 2007. Print. 5.

Back It Up

Read the passage above carefully. Couch is making a point about what makes a good Special Forces soldier. What point is he making? What are three pieces of evidence Couch uses to make that point? Write a paragraph describing Couch's main point and how he backs up his main idea.

CHAPTER FOUR

GREEN BERETS IN BATTLE

Life as a Green Beret can be tough. Green Beret units often work alone for long periods of time. They live with locals in a region. They learn their languages and customs. They build relationships with them. Green Berets often have little or no help from their superiors. The role of a Green Beret soldier has changed over time. Today their job has become even more dangerous.

Green Berets are trained to operate in places the army cannot go.

After the 2001 attacks on the United States, many Green Berets were sent to Iraq and other Middle Eastern countries.

On September 11, 2001, terrorists attacked the World Trade Center in New York City and the Pentagon in Washington DC. The US government made fighting terrorist groups an important priority. Violent groups exist throughout the world. But those responsible for the attack on the United States were being trained in Middle Eastern countries, such as Afghanistan and Iraq. And that's where the Green Berets were headed.

Green Berets in Iraq

In the spring of 2003, President George W. Bush launched an invasion of Iraq. US forces and their allies quickly defeated the Iraqi military. But the fighting was far from over. US forces stayed in the country to try to keep the peace. They needed to help Iraq set up a new government.

Green Berets worked with Iraqis. The Iraqi people needed protection from the Taliban. They were also in danger from Al Qaeda.

The Battle of Debecka Pass

The 3rd Special Forces Group participated in the 2003 invasion of Iraq. On April 6, 2003, the Green Berets spotted six Iraqi tanks in the distance. Suddenly the tanks began racing in their direction and firing. The Green Berets had a machine gun, rocket launcher, and plenty of ammunition. But they knew that their weapons were no match for the force of the tanks. Staff Sergeant Jason Brown placed his anti-tank missile on his shoulder. He fired and destroyed one of the tanks. But the Iraqis kept coming. The Green Berets pulled back to a spot known as Press Hill. The battle grew more intense. Brown hit three more tanks. He continued firing. Finally the Iraqis stopped their attack. The Green Berets had won.

Al Qaeda was the terrorist group that had claimed responsibility for attacking the United States. Both groups had also caused destruction and death in their own countries. The Green Berets taught the Iraqis how to defend their towns and villages. They met with local leaders to help them make their governments stronger. Strong city and state governments would have a better chance of standing up to terrorists.

Saddam Hussein had been the dictator of Iraq before the US invasion. The US government believed he

Humanitarian Work

Green Berets often take part in humanitarian work. They deliver food to starving villages. They provide medicine to those in need. They help people escape areas of intense fighting. Then they help these people settle in refugee camps away from the fighting. After the Vietnam War, Green Berets worked to disable dangerous land mines in Cambodia, a country near Vietnam. Green Berets have also worked to improve living conditions at home. In the 1970s, Green Berets worked to build hospitals and schools in rural areas of the United States.

Green Berets work with the locals in an area to learn about their concerns and teach them to defend themselves.

was supportive of terrorism. He was also cruel to the people of Iraq. US forces captured Hussein late in 2003. In 2006 he was executed.

Special Forces stayed in Iraq to try to make the country more stable. They wanted to make sure another dictator did not rise up to take Hussein's place. Even without Hussein, terrorist groups

The Green Berets' work in many different countries has helped make the world a safer place.

continued attacks across the country. Thanks to the Green Berets' training, Iraqis were able to fight back against these dangerous groups.

A Bright Future

The Green Berets' performance in combat for more than half a century has earned them many medals. Yet the most important mission of the Green Berets is earning the trust of people in need throughout the world. They are diplomats as well as soldiers. They will continue to learn other cultures and languages. Then they can train locals to defend themselves and their countries.

War has changed a lot since the birth of the Special Forces more than 60 years ago. Skilled combat troops are still required. But unconventional warriors such as the Green Berets could become more important than ever in future conflicts.

EXPLORE ONLINE

The focus of Chapter Four was Green Beret missions. The US Army Web site below discusses this same subject. As you know, every source is different. How is the information from the Web site different from the information given in this chapter? What information is the same? What can you learn from the Web site?

Primary Missions
www.goarmy.com/special-forces/primary-missions.html

IMPORTANT DATES AND BATTLES

1754–1763

Guerilla fighters during the French and Indian War start paving the way for Green Berets and their missions.

1861–1865

The Confederate Mosby's Raiders show what irregular soldiers can achieve during the Civil War.

1942

The Office of Strategic Services (OSS) is created to conduct special operations during World War II.

1961

President John F. Kennedy declares the green beret as the official headgear of the US Army Special Forces.

1968

Green Berets at the Lang Vei camp in Vietnam help themselves and villagers escape North Vietnamese soldiers.

1981

Green Berets are sent to El Salvador to help stop a Communist government.

1952

The army creates the first Special Forces unit, which is launched on June 19.

1953

Special Forces are sent to Germany to help Eastern Europeans rebel against their Communist governments.

1957

Special Forces teams go to the island of Okinawa, Japan, to help train the South Vietnamese army.

1990

Green Berets are sent to the Middle East to help free Kuwait from Iraq.

2001

Green Berets help defeat the Taliban in November to liberate the Afghan city of Mazar-e Sharif. It's the first major victory against the Taliban in Afghanistan.

2003

Green Berets stop the Iraqi advance on April 6 in the Battle of Debecka Pass.

Why Do I Care?

A Green Beret's life might not be as different from yours as you think. Have you ever been in a new place where you had to learn new customs? Have you ever needed to convince someone to trust you? Write down two or three ways the Green Berets connect to your life. How is your life similar to a Green Beret's?

Another View

There are many sources online and in your library about the Green Berets. Chapter Three of this book discusses Green Beret training. Ask a librarian or another adult to help you find a new source about Green Beret training. Then write a short essay comparing and contrasting the new source with this book. What points about Green Beret training do both authors make? What information is different between the two sources?

Say What?

Learning about Green Berets can mean learning a lot of new vocabulary. Find five words in this book that you have never seen or heard before. Use a dictionary to find out what they mean. Then write the meanings in your own words. Now use each word in a sentence.

You Are There

Imagine that you are a boy or girl living in a mountain village in Afghanistan. Green Berets have just arrived in your village to try to convince you to fight the Taliban. Do you trust the Green Berets? How do your parents and village leaders feel?

GLOSSARY

allies
soldiers or others working on the same side in a battle or war

communism
a system in which economic and social activities are controlled by the government

culture
the ways of people in a particular region or country

diplomat
a person who works to keep a good relationship with a different country

guerilla
a member of an irregular fighting force

infiltrate
sneak or force through enemy lines

liberate
remove people from enemy control, often through force

resistance
fight against enemy control

terrorist
a person or group that uses violence or the threat of violence to reach a goal

LEARN MORE

Books

David, Jack. *Army Green Berets*. Minneapolis: Bellwether, 2009.

Hamilton, John. *Green Berets (US Armed Forces)*. Minneapolis: ABDO & Daughters, 2011.

Hamilton, John. *Special Forces*. Edina, MN: ABDO, 2007.

Web Links

To learn more about Green Berets, visit ABDO Publishing Company online at **www.abdopublishing.com**. Web sites about Green Berets are featured on our Book Links page. These links are routinely monitored and updated to provide the most current information available.

Visit **www.mycorelibrary.com** for free additional tools for teachers and students.

INDEX

ABOUT THE AUTHOR

Martin Gitlin is a freelance writer based in Cleveland, Ohio. He has written more than 60 educational books. Gitlin has won more than 45 awards during his 30 years as a writer, including first place for general excellence from the Associated Press. He lives with his wife and three children.